THE OFFICIAL Arsenal ANNUAL 2022

g

A Grange Publication

TM © (2021) The Arsenal Football Club plc.
All rights reserved.

Manufactured and distributed under licence by Grange Communications Ltd., Edinburgh. Printed in the EU.

Photographs © Arsenal Football Club, Alamy and Shutterstock.

ISBN 978-1-913578-64-0

CONTENTS

WELCOME!

Last season was the strangest one anybody can remember, with no fans allowed at most of the matches – we missed them so much.

I've always said that the fans are the soul of this club and we need them next to us. We knew that before, but we realise it even more now. The impact the fans have cannot be quantified. We don't know what it is, but it is so powerful.

I feel that after being apart from our fans on matchdays for so long, that our bond has actually grown stronger in that time. We all need that connection – the players and the fans – and I know the team feeds off the energy, the belief and the positivity the supporters bring.

It's what football is. Arsenal is a family, and there's nothing like being reunited with people you have missed. It is a unique feeling – the fans can make you feel unstoppable, they offer us protection, and it's the reason I am looking forward to our future together. Back with you all – the fans – right behind us.

We are proud of our fans, and we want our fans to be proud of the team. That's my job, that's my objective. As manager of the club, it's up to me to deliver something on the pitch that excites you all.

And I feel we are building a squad that can do that. During the summer we worked hard as a club to bring in some very talented players who have certainly made the squad much stronger.

We brought in Nuno Tavares, Sambi Lokonga, Ben White, Martin Odegaard, Aaron Ramsdale and Takehiro Tomiyasu and for me what's most pleasing is that although all six are ready for the first team now, we signed all of them while they have their best years ahead of them.

All six were 23 or under when they signed, and I'm excited to see how they all develop in Arsenal colours over the next few seasons.

We all have a clear vision of where we want this club to go – now we want to deliver.

So enjoy the book, keep getting behind us, and let's move forward together.

MIKEL ARTETA

ROLL OF HONOUR

League champions: 1931, 1933, 1934, 1935, 1938, 1948, 1953, 1971, 1989, 1991, 1998, 2002, 2004
FA Cup winners: 1930, 1936, 1950, 1971, 1979, 1993, 1998, 2002, 2003, 2005, 2014, 2015, 2017, 2020

League Cup winners: 1987, 1993
European Fairs Cup winners: 1970
European Cup Winners' Cup winners: 1994
Charity/Community Shield winners: 1930, 1931, 1933, 1934, 1938, 1948, 1953, 1991 (shared), 1998, 1999, 2002, 2004, 2014, 2015, 2017, 2020

2020-2021
SEASON REVIEW

August

The celebratory confetti had barely settled on the Wembley pitch after the glorious FA Cup final at the start of the month, when we were back at the national stadium for the Community Shield against champions Liverpool. Pierre-Emerick Aubameyang picked up where he left off in the final, with another great goal to put us ahead early on. Liverpool hit back to take the game to penalties but Aubameyang struck the winning spot kick to earn more silverware, and get the new campaign off to a flying start.

RESULTS

Sat 29 Community Shield
Liverpool (Wembley)
1-1 *Aubameyang*
(Arsenal won 5-4 on pens)

THE FA
COMMUNITY SHIELD

September

The Gunners began the league season with a swagger against newly promoted Fulham. It took just eight minutes for us to get up and running, through Alexandre Lacazette, with Brazilian defender Gabriel marking his debut with a goal in the second half. Aubameyang sealed the points in style, crashing home from long range, a few days before agreeing a new long-term deal with the club. Our first home game of the season was another London derby, and it took a late Eddie Nketiah winner to grab all three points. England Under-21 star, Nketiah, then scored again late on against Leicester to ensure we progressed in the Carabao Cup, and extended our unbeaten start to the season. That run came to an end at Anfield though, despite Lacazette giving us the lead with his third goal in three league games.

RESULTS

Sat 12 Premier League
Fulham (A)
3-0 *Lacazette, Gabriel, Aubameyang*

Sat 19 Premier League
West Ham United (H)
2-1 *Lacazette, Nketiah*

Wed 23 Carabao Cup
Leicester City (A)
2-0 *Fuchs (og), Nketiah*

Mon 28 Premier League
Liverpool (A)
1-3 *Lacazette*

October

We were back at Anfield just three days later, and this time we emerged victorious after another penalty shoot-out. Neither side could find a goal in regulation time, but once again we kept our nerve from 12 yards, while Bernd Leno made two saves, and we progressed into the last eight of the Carabao Cup. We were back to winning ways in the league as well, thanks to Bukayo Saka and Nicolas Pepe's first goals of the campaign at home to Sheffield United. Then came back-to-back 1-0 defeats though that checked our progress. The first was away to Manchester City – in a game which saw Thomas Partey make his debut – then at home to Leicester, losing out to a late Jamie Vardy strike.

There was positive news in Europe though. We began the Europa League group stage with solid victories away to Rapid Vienna then at home against Irish side Dundalk. Pepe scored a screamer to seal a 3-0 win in the latter and put us top of the group.

RESULTS

Thur 1 Carabao Cup
Liverpool (A)
0-0
(Arsenal won 5-4 on pens)

Sun 4 Premier League
Sheffield United (H)
2-1 *Saka, Pepe*

Sat 17 Premier League
Manchester City (A)
0-1

Thur 22 Europa League
Rapid Vienna (A)
2-1 *David Luiz, Aubameyang*

Sun 25 Premier League
Leicester City (A)
0-1

Thur 29 Europa League
Dundalk (H)
3-0 *Nketiah, Willock, Pepe*

November

A second-half penalty from Aubameyang gave us a thoroughly deserved victory away to Manchester United – our first Premier League win at Old Trafford for 14 years. Partey was particularly impressive in midfield as we rose above United – as well as Manchester City and Tottenham – just behind the early pacesetters in the table. But poor results against Aston Villa, Leeds United and Wolves soon dropped us into the bottom half. Villa triumphed 3-0 at the Emirates and after the international break, a red card for Pepe limited us to just a goalless draw away to Leeds. We were finding goals hard to come by in the league, and although we netted at home to Wolves, they hit back to win 2-1, in a game marred by a sickening head injury sustained by visiting striker Raul Jimenez, that would rule him out for the season.

But if we were struggling in domestic competition, we went from strength to strength in Europe, recording thumping home and away wins over Norwegian side Molde to book our place in the knock-out stages yet again. Exciting young academy striker Folarin Balogun netted in the away match – his first goal at senior level.

RESULTS

Sun 1 Premier League
Manchester United (A)
1-0 *Aubameyang (pen)*

Thur 5 Europa League
Molde (H)
4-1 *Haugen (og), Sinyan (og), Pepe, Willock*

Sun 8 Premier League
Aston Villa (H)
0-3

Sun 22 Premier League
Leeds United (A)
0-0

Thur 26 Europa League
Molde (A)
3-0 *Pepe, Nelson, Balogun*

Sun 29 Premier League
Wolves (H)
1-2 *Gabriel*

Arsenal.com
Player of the Month GABRIEL

December

There was the very welcome sight of fans back inside Emirates Stadium for our Europa League group stage match against Rapid Vienna. We had played all home games behind closed doors since last March – meaning our fans had been locked out for 271 days. And although only 2,000 were allowed in to see us beat Rapid 4-1, it felt like a significant step. There were fans too at the first north London derby of the season, but two breakaway goals for the hosts made it an afternoon to forget. We completed a 100 per cent record in the Europa League group stage with another high-scoring win over Dundalk, but our poor league form continued. Aubameyang scored an unfortunate own goal late on against Burnley at home after Granit Xhaka had earlier seen red. But it was Aubameyang to the rescue in the next game at home to Southampton – equalising former Gunner Theo Walcott's earlier goal. We finished the game with ten men though for the second successive match, after defender Gabriel was sent off. We were unable to build on that point against the Saints, losing 2-1 away to Everton before Manchester City ended our Carabao Cup hopes at the quarter-final stage, running out 4-1 winners at the Emirates. Mikel Arteta's men were therefore under huge pressure going into the Boxing Day match at home to Chelsea. And they responded in fine style, earning an excellent 3-1 win. Emile Smith Rowe, making his first league start of the season, particularly caught the eye, as did Xhaka with a wonderful free-kick, and Saka with a curler into the far corner to make it three. We followed it up with a win away to Brighton – courtesy of Lacazette's seventh of the season – to finish a busy month, and indeed a hectic 2020, on a high.

Arsenal.com **Player of the Month** BUKAYO **SAKA**

RESULTS

Thur 3 Europa League
Rapid Vienna (H)
4-1 *Lacazette, Mari, Nketiah, Smith Rowe*

Sun 6 Premier League
Tottenham Hotspur (A)
0-2

Thur 10 Europa League
Dundalk (A)
4-2 *Nketiah, Elneny, Willock, Balogun*

Sun 13 Premier League
Burnley (H)
0-1

Wed 16 Premier League
Southampton (H)
1-1 *Aubameyang*

Sat 19 Premier League
Everton (A)
1-2 *Pepe (pen)*

Tue 22 Carabao Cup
Manchester City (H)
1-4 *Lacazette*

Sat 26 Premier League
Chelsea (H)
3-1 *Lacazette (pen), Xhaka, Saka*

Tue 29 Premier League
Brighton & Hove Albion (A)
1-0 *Lacazette*

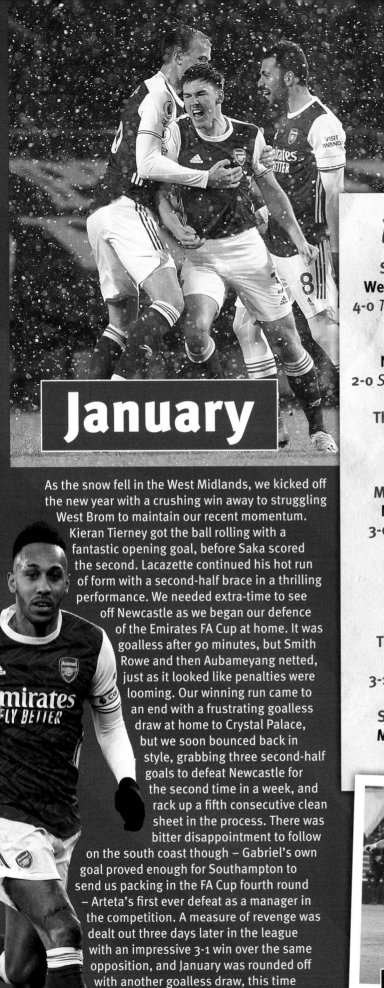

January

As the snow fell in the West Midlands, we kicked off the new year with a crushing win away to struggling West Brom to maintain our recent momentum. Kieran Tierney got the ball rolling with a fantastic opening goal, before Saka scored the second. Lacazette continued his hot run of form with a second-half brace in a thrilling performance. We needed extra-time to see off Newcastle as we began our defence of the Emirates FA Cup at home. It was goalless after 90 minutes, but Smith Rowe and then Aubameyang netted, just as it looked like penalties were looming. Our winning run came to an end with a frustrating goalless draw at home to Crystal Palace, but we soon bounced back in style, grabbing three second-half goals to defeat Newcastle for the second time in a week, and rack up a fifth consecutive clean sheet in the process. There was bitter disappointment to follow on the south coast though – Gabriel's own goal proved enough for Southampton to send us packing in the FA Cup fourth round – Arteta's first ever defeat as a manager in the competition. A measure of revenge was dealt out three days later in the league with an impressive 3-1 win over the same opposition, and January was rounded off with another goalless draw, this time against title-chasing Manchester United.

RESULTS

Sat 2 Premier League
West Bromwich Albion (A)
4-0 *Tierney, Saka, Lacazette 2*

Sat 9 FA Cup
Newcastle United (H)
2-0 *Smith Rowe, Aubameyang*

Thur 14 Premier League
Crystal Palace (H)
0-0

Mon 18 Premier League
Newcastle United (H)
3-0 *Aubameyang 2, Saka*

Sat 23 FA Cup
Southampton (A)
0-1

Tue 26 Premier League
Southampton (A)
3-1 *Pepe, Saka, Lacazette*

Sat 30 Premier League
Manchester United (H)
0-0

Arsenal.com
Player of the Month
BUKAYO
SAKA

13

February

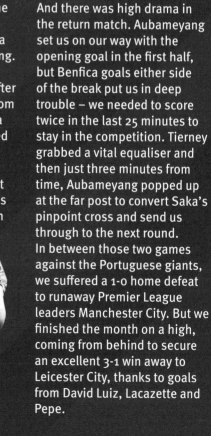

RESULTS

Tue 2 Premier League
Wolves (A)
1-2 *Pepe*

Sat 6 Premier League
Aston Villa (A)
0-1

Sun 14 Premier League
Leeds United (H)
4-2
Aubameyang 3 (1 pen), Bellerin

Thur 18 Europa League
Benfica (A)
1-1 *Saka*

Sun 21 Premier League
Manchester City (H)
0-1

Thur 25 Europa League
Benfica (H)
3-2 *Aubameyang 2,
Tierney*

Sun 28 Premier League
Leicester City (A)
3-1 *David Luiz,
Lacazette (pen), Pepe*

We looked to be well on course for victory at Wolves, after a mesmerising first-half display featuring a cracking goal from Pepe. But David Luiz was sent off in first-half injury time, and the hosts scored the resulting penalty to transform the game. The winner came in the second half and Bernd Leno was also later dismissed on a thoroughly frustrating evening. We suffered another narrow defeat in our next match – after we were unable to recover from a second-minute goal at Villa Park. But Aubameyang scored his first ever Premier League hat-trick to get us back to winning ways at home to Leeds United. Then attention switched back to the Europa League, and a meeting with Benfica in the Round of 32 – staged in Rome due to Covid regulations. Saka's equaliser meant we had a valuable 'away' goal to take into the second leg, to be played in Greece. And there was high drama in the return match. Aubameyang set us on our way with the opening goal in the first half, but Benfica goals either side of the break put us in deep trouble – we needed to score twice in the last 25 minutes to stay in the competition. Tierney grabbed a vital equaliser and then just three minutes from time, Aubameyang popped up at the far post to convert Saka's pinpoint cross and send us through to the next round. In between those two games against the Portuguese giants, we suffered a 1-0 home defeat to runaway Premier League leaders Manchester City. But we finished the month on a high, coming from behind to secure an excellent 3-1 win away to Leicester City, thanks to goals from David Luiz, Lacazette and Pepe.

March

A frantic finale – in which we hit the post and had a strong penalty appeal turned down – was not enough to take maximum points against Burnley, despite us dominating large periods of the game. Aubameyang's 14th goal of the season had given us an early lead, but Burnley's Chris Wood benefitted from a defensive error to level. Another defensive mix-up threatened to cost us dear in the Europa League Round of 16 first leg away to Olympiacos, after Martin Odegaard had put us ahead with his first goal for the club. Late goals from Gabriel and Mohamed Elneny put us firmly in charge of the tie however. Odegaard was on target again in our next match – the north London derby – and Lacazette struck the winner from the penalty spot to seal a comeback victory over our local rivals. We progressed to the last eight of the Europa League despite a 1-0 home defeat in the second leg against Olympiacos, before an action-packed league fixture at West Ham's London Stadium. We found ourselves 3-0 down after 32 minutes against the Hammers, before staging a spirited fightback. Lacazette's snap shot was turned into his own net by Tomas Soucek before a Calum Chambers cross was deflected in by Craig Dawson for another own goal. Lacazette headed the equaliser late on, and we even came close to taking maximum points during an incredible finale.

RESULTS

Sat 6 Premier League
Burnley (A)
1-1 *Aubameyang*

Thur 11 Europa League
Olympiacos (A)
3-1 *Odegaard, Gabriel, Elneny*

Sun 14 Premier League
Tottenham Hotspur (H)
2-1 *Odegaard, Lacazette (pen)*

Thur 18 Europa League
Olympiacos (H)
0-1

Sun 21 Premier League
West Ham United (A)
3-3 *Soucek (og), Dawson (og), Lacazette*

Arsenal.com
Player of the Month
MARTIN **ODEGAARD**

April

Liverpool ran out comfortable 3-0 winners in another disappointing behind closed doors game at the Emirates before we resumed our Europa League campaign at home to Slavia Prague in the quarter-final. All the action came in the final five minutes. Pepe finally gave us the lead late on, only for the Czech side to snatch a huge equaliser in the last seconds of injury-time. We warmed up for the all-important return match in Prague with a comfortable 3-0 win away to Sheffield United in the league, with Lacazette grabbing a brace. Needing to score at least once away to Slavia to progress, we stormed in to a three-goal lead inside 24 minutes, thanks to some devastating attacking play. Smith Rowe had already had a goal disallowed before Pepe gave us the lead on 18 minutes – signalling the start of the onslaught. Lacazette doubled the lead from the penalty spot and livewire Saka increased the advantage moments later with an excellent finish. Lacazette capped a memorable night with the fourth late on. It was back to league action at home to Fulham, and Nketiah rescued a point with an equaliser at the death, but there were no late heroics against Everton, and Leno's unfortunate own goal condemned us to defeat. We travelled to Spain for our third Europa League semi-final appearance of the past four years – this time against former boss Unai Emery's Villarreal side. The hosts raced into a two-goal lead, and our task was made even harder following a red card to Dani Ceballos. But Pepe kept his cool to grab an away goal from the penalty spot and ensure the tie was finely poised for the return match in London.

RESULTS

Sat 3 Premier League
Liverpool (H)
0-3

Thur 8 Europa League
Slavia Prague (H)
1-1 *Pepe*

Sun 11 Premier League
Sheffield United (A)
3-0 *Lacazette 2, Martinelli*

Thur 15 Europa League
Slavia Prague (A)
4-0 *Pepe, Lacazette 2 (1 pen), Saka*

Sun 18 Premier League
Fulham (H)
1-1 *Nketiah*

Fri 23 Premier League
Everton (H)
0-1

Thur 29 Europa League
Villarreal (A)
1-2 *Pepe (pen)*

Arsenal.com/mem[

Arsenal.com
**Player of
the Month**
ALEXANDRE
LACAZETTE

May

Elneny scored his first ever Premier League goal as we returned to winning ways at St James's Park, before the crunch second leg against Villarreal at the Emirates. A 1-0 win would have been enough for us to reach the final, but we could just not find a way through Emery's well-organised side, and despite hitting the woodwork twice through Aubameyang, we crashed out of the competition with a goalless draw. It left us facing up to the prospect of no European football next season. But a strong finish in the Premier League meant we took that fight for European qualification all the way to the last whistle of the season. Smith Rowe scored his first Premier League goal in the home win over West Brom – with Willian scoring a superb free-kick to open his Gunners account too. Smith Rowe made it back-to-back goals by grabbing the winner at Stamford Bridge, and there was last drama in our final away game of the season. Fans were allowed back into the stadium for the match at Crystal Palace, but Pepe silenced them with a superb opening goal. It looked like we would be denied all three points after the hosts equalised, only for Gabriel Martinelli – and Pepe again – to net in injury-time to keep European qualification alive. So it came to the final day, in front of 10,000 returning fans at the Emirates. Pepe kept up his hot run of form with two more well-taken goals to take his seasonal tally to 16, but results elsewhere went against us, meaning we finished eighth for the second season running, despite earning five more points than last term.

RESULTS

Sun 2 Premier League
Newcastle United (A)
2-0 *Elneny, Aubameyang*

Thur 6 Europa League
Villarreal (H)
0-0

Sun 9 Premier League
West Bromwich Albion (H)
3-1 *Smith Rowe, Pepe, Willian*

Wed 12
Premier League
Chelsea (A)
1-0 *Smith Rowe*

Wed 19 Premier League
Crystal Palace (A)
3-1 *Pepe 2, Martinelli*

Sun 23 Premier League
Brighton & Hove Albion (H)
2-0 *Pepe 2*

Arsenal.com
**Player of
the Season**
BUKAYO
SAKA

17

PLAYER SPOTLIGHT

3
DEF

KIERAN TIERNEY

A whole-hearted, committed defender, Kieran has quickly become a firm fans' favourite since joining from Celtic in 2019. An attack-minded, indefatigable left back, Kieran had another excellent season last term, contributing four assists and two vital goals, as well as his usual solid displays at the back. He scored his first of the 2020/21 season in the 4-0 win at West Brom, then grabbed a vital goal away to Benfica in the Europa League. A serial winner, he won four Scottish Premier League titles, two Scottish FA Cups and two Scottish League Cups at Celtic, all before the age of 22, when he made the move to London. He has been a regular for Scotland since his teenage years, and starred at Euro 2020 in summer 2021.

Born: Douglas, Isle of Man, June 5, 1997
Nationality: Scottish
Joined Arsenal: from Celtic, August 8, 2019
Previous club: Celtic
Debut: v Nottingham Forest (h), League Cup, September 24, 2019 (won 5-0)

PLAYER SPOTLIGHT

7
FWD

BUKAYO SAKA

One of the most gifted players of his generation, Bukayo had another stand-out season for the Gunners, to be voted our Player of the Year – while still a teenager. He notched seven goals in all competitions, and the same number of assists – no player had more for us in 2020/21. Usually deployed as a dangerous wide forward – capable of deciding a game with a moment of magic, he's also proved his versatility in recent years, impressing at full-back, comfortable on either flank. A product of the Arsenal Academy, Bukayo has been with us from the age of eight and started this season approaching a century of appearances for the first-team. A full England international, he featured at Euro 2020, becoming the country's youngest-ever player to feature in a major final.

Born: Ealing, London, September 5, 2001
Nationality: English
Joined Arsenal: as a full-time scholar in July 2018
Previous clubs: none
Debut: v Vorskla Poltava (a), Europa League, November 29, 2018 (won 3-0)
First goal: v Eintracht Frankfurt (a), Europa League, September 19, 2019 (won 3-0)

HIGHER OR LOWER?

Can you work out what symbol should go next to each player in this name chain so that they are in order of Premier League appearances? The first one has been done for you.

Answers on page 61

Cesc Fabregas

HIGHER - HENRY MADE MORE PREMIER LEAGUE APPEARANCES THAN FABREGAS

Freddie Ljungberg

Thierry Henry

Tony Adams

Dennis Bergkamp

Laurent Koscielny

Patrick Vieira

Robert Pires

20

ODD ONE OUT

Who's the odd one out in these following groups?

1. Per Mertesacker, Robin van Persie, Patrick Vieira, Cesc Fabregas, Emmanuel Petit

2. William Gallas, Dennis Bergkamp, Mesut Ozil, Santi Cazorla, Jack Wilshere

3. Bukayo Saka, Emile Smith Rowe, Rob Holding, Reiss Nelson, Ainsley Maitland-Niles

4. Sead Kolasinac, Pierre-Emerick Aubameyang, Gabriel Magalhaes, Gabriel Martinelli, Cedric Soares

5. Arsène Wenger, Unai Emery, Mikel Arteta, George Graham, Herbert Chapman

6. Old Trafford, White Hart Lane, Anfield, Etihad Stadium, Stamford Bridge

7. Alexis Sanchez, Thierry Henry, Olivier Giroud, Theo Walcott, Dennis Bergkamp

8. Hector Bellerin, Mesut Ozil, Robin van Persie, Nicolas Pepe, Lukas Podolski

9. Fly Emirates, EA Sports, JVC, O2, SEGA

10. 2001/02, 1997/98, 1990/91, 2003/04, 1999/2000

PICTURE PERFECT!

Catching up with what our players have been posting to Instagram – give them a follow!

Ben White @ben_white6

My new home. Can't wait to get started @arsenal

Pierre-Emerick Aubameyang @auba

🏝️Sunset🏝️

Sambi Lokonga @sambilokonga48

What a feeling to play at the Emirates stadium and to meet you guys … ASL23 x AS48 #YaDieudedans! Que du chemin parcouru !

Folarin Balogun @balogun

My home. My heart
See you soon Gunners 🖤
#Balogun2025

Thomas Partey @thomaspartey5

Boat ride 🧑🏿✈️⚓

Nuno Tavares @nuno_tavares71

Ready to go 21/22 @arsenal

22

Bernd Leno @berndleno01

Thank you for all the birthday wishes 👍 😃 🎂

Emile Smith-Rowe @emilesmithrowe

🖊
New season.
New contract.
New number.

Granit Xhaka @granitxhaka

This amazing journey comes to an end and trust me, it really hurts. But I couldn't be prouder of this group. We are a squad of brothers. All of us. We win together. We lose together. It's an honour to play with these guys and we're going to come back stronger from this 💪 🇨🇭 #HoppSchwiiz #Xhaka

Nicolas Pepe @nicolas.pepe19

NP19 🚀

Bukayo Saka @bukayosaka87

This was amazing to come back to! I want to thank everyone who has sent me supportive messages and gifts. I've seen, read and appreciate every one of you. I hope we all continue to spread love and joy 🙏

Kiernan Tierney @kierantierney

I'm proud to be an ambassador for Scotland's animal welfare charity the Scottish SPCA. In 2020, they responded to 78,000 reports of animals in need which is over 210 every day. They rehomed almost 4,000 animals and released over 3,000 wild animals back to the wild. I'm looking forward to working with their special investigations unit to help raise awareness of crimes against animals. @official_scottishspca

PLAYER SPOTLIGHT

Born: Laval, France, June 18, 1989
Nationality: Gabonese
Joined Arsenal: from Borussia Dortmund on January 31, 2018
Previous clubs: AC Milan, Dijon (loan), Lille (loan), Monaco (loan), Saint-Etienne, Borussia Dortmund
Debut: v Everton (h), Premier League, February 3, 2018 (won 5-1)
First goal: v Everton (h), Premier League, February 3, 2018 (won 5-1)

14
FWD

PIERRE-EMERICK AUBAMEYANG

One of the world's most deadly strikers, Auba – as he is known around the club – began this season closing in on a century of goals for the Gunners. The Premier League Golden Boot winner in 2018/19, the Gabon forward ended the following campaign – his first full season as club captain – by lifting the FA Cup, after scoring both goals in the final against Chelsea at Wembley. Although last season was disrupted by illness, he again reached double figures in the Premier League, including his first ever hat-trick for the club, in the 4-2 home win over Leeds United in February 2021. A livewire, ebullient figure in the dressing room, Auba signed a new long-term contract at the start of 2020/21, and continues to lead by example. An explosive forward who can play wide on the left or as centre forward, he captains the Gabon national team, and helped them qualify for the 2021 Africa Cup of Nations.

32
GK

AARON RAMSDALE

Talented young goalkeeper Aaron has been named Player of the Season in each of the past three years – at three different clubs. First he won Young Player of the Year while on loan at AFC Wimbledon in 2018/19, then the following season starred for Bournemouth in the Premier League, earning the Supporters' Player of the Year honour. Then last season, having moved back to his first club Sheffield United, he was ever-present in the Premier League, and won both Player and Young Player of the Year for the club. That helped the modern-style keeper earn an England call-up for Euro 2020, though he didn't feature at the tournament. Aaron has tasted success for his country before though, keeping three clean sheets from five appearances when helping England win the Under-19 European Championships in 2017. He also played regularly for the

Born: Stoke-on-Trent, May 14, 1998
Nationality: English
Joined Arsenal: from Sheffield United on August 20, 2021
Previous clubs: Bournemouth, Chesterfield (loan), AFC Wimbledon (loan),

LIFE AFTER FOOTBALL

What do our players intend to do when they hang up their boots? We asked them all to find out!

 EMILE SMITH ROWE

I've not really thought about it yet. I've got lots of little cousins and I love playing football with them so I'd definitely like to get involved in coaching kids or something like that. Apart from that I really want to travel. I don't get much time for that during the season, but it's something I want to do in my life in the future. There are so many places that I want to see. It sounds really bad but first of all I've never seen the Eiffel Tower, so I need to visit there at some point. That should be an easy one to tick off! Maybe that's one for next summer. Other than that I want to go to Brazil and a few places in America.

 NICOLAS PEPE

I would like to be a coach or a manager. I have started my qualifications already in fact, I have passed one but it's just the basic one. So I haven't looked into it in any detail yet, but it's a start. It doesn't necessarily mean it will lead into coaching by the way. It can do, but it can also lead into a more general football management role, but as I said, I am not focussed on that at the moment.

 GABRIEL MARTINELLI

Wow! It's too soon, but I don't think I'd be a coach. You can never say never, but thinking about it now, at 20, I don't think I would be a manager. So far, I have no plans for the end of my career. Before that I have big plans and dreams. I want to work hard and give all I can to be the best in the world. To play for Brazil, win the Champions League, win a World Cup. I dream of all that.

 **PABLO MARI**

When I finish playing I'd like to concentrate on my investments. I have a few properties and flats that I rent so I will manage that. I also have investments in other parts of my business that I will manage. Also, I would like to work with my agent, and bring some football experience to him in his business. Most agents haven't played football so they don't know that side of the business well and what happens in the dressing room. So I think I can bring that to the company and I really like working with them anyway – it's a really good company.

 THOMAS PARTEY

I have a lot of plans because I know this isn't going to last forever! I love football and it will always be part of my life so I would love to stay close to it and include it in what I do. So maybe I will be a coach or something else, whatever keeps me close to the game. I haven't started any coaching qualifications yet, but I've played for some good coaches in my career, and all of them I've worked with since I was young, I try to learn a lot from them all. I'm sure that before I end my career I'll be able to know more about coaching. Also, when I stop playing I'd like to study and get a degree. An administrative or business degree maybe, a course that teaches you more about business and the life you live. I want to start that soon, I've got a plan and I want to get a place where I can study whenever I'm free. I can hopefully fit it around my football schedule.

CALUM CHAMBERS

I had never really thought about it much before, but during lockdown and when I was injured last year, it made me think more. I had a lot of time to do some deep thinking and one of the things I thought about was just that: 'What am I going to do when I retire?' Obviously I love football so I thought 'Why wouldn't I want to stay in the sport?' So I got in contact with a few people to start the process of doing my coaching badges. I reached out to Per Mertesacker for some contacts to get the ball rolling on that, so at the moment I'm thinking it could be some coaching somewhere, staying in the game, but I really don't know where – maybe an academy or something. Also, I've always wanted to travel. At the start of every year I always say to myself that I want to go and see a new place. That's what I'm looking forward to doing when I retire. I haven't travelled enough.

ROB HOLDING

My plan is to be on a beach somewhere on the coast of California! Literally the plan is to play my last few years of my career in the MLS then retire, with my coaching badges. Then I want to get a coaching job where that isn't pressured like the Premier League, then I can just enjoy it and help kids get better and live in the Sunshine State where life is good. I feel like you go through 15 years of pressure as a footballer, I don't want to have another 15 years being scrutinised as a manager. I'd rather enjoy it somewhere where I'm not judged and nobody has an opinion on me! Literally retire to a little beach house and not been seen again by anyone - perfect!

KIERAN TIERNEY

Well, when I finish playing I'll be back in Scotland, no doubt going back to my old life of supporting Celtic home and away again! I'll be back there doing something anyway. I'll definitely live in Scotland when I finish playing, 100 per cent, I miss it every day.

BERND LENO

No, I have absolutely no idea! I don't know what will happen in the future, maybe we will have kids, so things could be completely different. But I think we will probably settle back in Germany. Probably back in my home town of Stuttgart, or around there. I'm interested to stay in football maybe, but I don't know if that will be in professional football, or with youth teams. Maybe I could play with my friends in a small Sunday team, or be a manager at that level. But the one thing I want to do is travel. There is so much in the world to see, so many beautiful places. Also, when I retire I want to go skiing – in Austria or somewhere like that. When I was a child I never got the chance to go skiing in Switzerland or Austria, and then when I was older it was too dangerous to do in case of injury. But everybody says it's amazing, so it's one thing I want to learn after my career.

GRANIT XHAKA

Of course, I'm not the youngest anymore, I'm 29 now and when I see Eddie, Emile and Bukayo I realise that! So I want to do my coaching licence soon, I think I will start that this year. But my dream is to be a sporting director at a club, for example like Edu. But also I want to become a manager like Mikel because I love that part of football. I like to speak to players and work with them, so let's see if it works in the future. But that would be step one, to be a coach, but my big dream is to be a sporting director. To do that job you have people around you that you need to speak to about a player for example, what is best for the team, the club. I love that side of it, to build something together and create relationships.

ALEXANDRE LACAZETTE

I can definitely tell you that I won't be doing media work – it's not for me! I don't find it easy to talk during a game or afterwards about what players have been doing. Maybe I would like to coach at an academy or be part of the coaching staff at a club, but not as a main coach, because I think that's a really hard job. There is a lot of stress on that job and I think after my playing career I would like to enjoy football more without so much pressure on it, that comes from everywhere. So that's why maybe I would like to do youth team coaching, because that is much more about football itself, towards coaching, learning and being able to teach young players. I would prefer to do that than be a first-team manager.

PLAYER SPOTLIGHT

5
MID

THOMAS PARTEY

A powerful, imposing figure in the middle of the pitch, Thomas gave a number of stand-out performances during his debut season at Arsenal. Arriving from Atletico Madrid at the start of the season, the Ghanaian midfielder was soon making his mark in the Premier League, turning in a man-of-the-match display in the 1-0 win at Old Trafford. A ball-winner with the ability to dominate games, Thomas won the Europa League and European Super Cup with his previous side, and played in the 2016 Champions League final. Overall he spent five seasons in the Spanish capital, earning a reputation as one of the league's star players. Named Ghana's Player of the Year in both 2018 and 2019, he remains a mainstay of the national side, and has twice featured at the Africa Cup of Nations.

Born: Krobo Odumase, Ghana, June 13, 1993
Nationality: Ghanaian
Joined Arsenal: from Atletico Madrid on October 5, 2020
Previous clubs: Atletico Madrid, Mallorca (loan), Almeria (loan)
Debut: v Manchester City (a), Premier League, October 17, 2020 (lost 0-1)

PLAYER SPOTLIGHT

19
FWD

NICOLAS PEPE

A tricky, incredibly skilful winger, Nico scored 16 goals in all competitions last term – including some absolute crackers. The Ivory Coast international also added six assists, as he continued to grow in influence in the Gunners side. Arriving from Lille as a club record signing in 2019, he scored eight goals in his debut season, but went up a level last year. He ended the campaign with braces in our last two matches, and tormented defences with his trickery. Fast and direct, Nico usually likes to cut in on his left foot from the right wing, but can play on either flank, and is also a dead ball specialist. He was Lille's Player of the Season in 2018/19, and remains an important part of the Ivory Coast national side.

Born: Mantes-la-Jolie, France, May 29, 1995
Nationality: Ivorian
Joined Arsenal: from Lille on August 1, 2019
Previous clubs: Poitiers, Angers, Orleans (loan), Lille
Debut: v Newcastle United (a), Premier League, August 11, 2019 (won 1-0)
First goal: v Aston Villa (h), Premier League, September 22, 2019 (won 3-2)

KIM LITTLE

LYDIA WILLIAMS

ARSENAL WOMEN AT THE OLYMPICS

There were eight Arsenal players in action at the Tokyo Olympics in the summer, with star Dutch striker *Vivianne Miedema* finishing as the tournament's top scorer with ten goals from just four matches.

Miedema scored four in the opening group game against Zambia, then two more in a thrilling 3-3 draw with Brazil. Netherlands finished Group F with an 8-2 win over

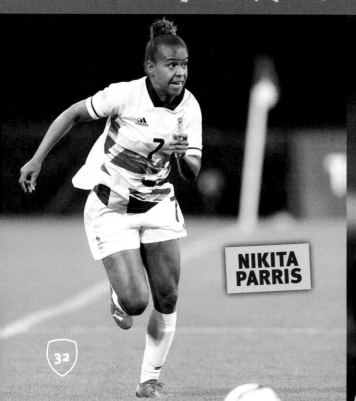

NIKITA PARRIS

VIVIANNE MIEDEMA

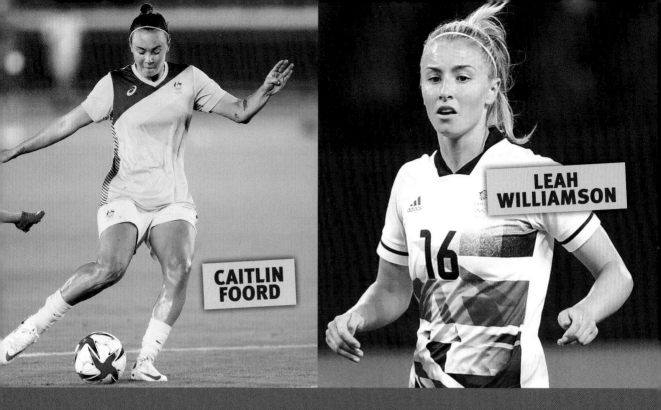

CAITLIN FOORD

LEAH WILLIAMSON

China, in which Miedema scored another brace. It took them through to a quarter-final meeting with USA, and although Miedema scored two more, the Americans progressed on penalties after a 2-2 draw.

USA went on to beat Australia in the bronze medal match. Arsenal's Caitlin Foord scored in that game, but America triumphed 4-3. Goalkeeper Lydia Williams and defender Steph Catley were also in the Australian squad.

And it was the Aussies who put paid to Great Britain's hopes at the quarter-final stage. There were three Gunners representing Team GB – defender Leah Williamson, new signing Nikita Parris and Scottish star Kim Little. It was a former Gunner who stole the show though – Ellen White grabbed six goals to be joint second top scorer.

The eighth Arsenal player starring in Tokyo was Mana Iwabuchi, who represented the home nation, and scored their first goal of the tournament. Japan also exited at the last eight stage.

Iwabuchi is another new signing who – along with Parris, Frida Maanum and Simone Boye Sorensen – joined the club in the summer to bolster Jonas Eidevall's squad for 2021/22.

STEPH CATLEY

MANA IWABUCHI

WELCOME TO ARSENAL,
JONAS!

Arsenal Women have a new boss this season – Swede Jonas Eidevall.

Previously the manager of Rosengard in his home country, he helped the Malmo club reach the quarter-finals of last season's Women's Champions League.

He won back-to-back league titles in 2013 and 2014, and another in 2019 – building a reputation as one of the most forward-thinking young managers in the game.

He was appointed shortly before the start of the season, and the 38 year old said: "I feel honoured to be taking this role. Arsenal have a rich history, more successful than any other women's team in England. I want to add to these honours.

"It's super important that we win, and we will be very ambitious about that, but it's even more important that we live the values and defend the club badge on a day-to-day basis.

"The ambitions that the club has, they want to be a world-leading team inside women's

EIDEVALL FACTFILE

Born: January 28, 1983, Boras, Sweden
Joined Arsenal: June 28, 2021
Clubs as a coach: Lunds BK (men's), Rosengard
Honours: Swedish women's league championship 2013, 2014, 2019, Swedish Cup winners 2018

football and that's obviously what attracts me, that they want to win both the Women's Champions League and the title in England.

"Of course, it's also about the way we want to achieve success and that the club has a clear philosophy and a way of playing and we want to achieve success through that. That really excites me, also that it's a club with a rich history.

"It's the most successful women's team in England and obviously through the growth now of the women's game, a lot of different teams are also coming up, but I can tell from listening in to the people at the club that the club right now are making major investments into the women's team.

"It's always about understanding the club's ambition. Where are they now and where do they want to be in the future? Then I want to see myself in that picture and see whether I can be the right person leading this team and getting it where the club wants it to be."

...AND THANKS FOR EVERYTHING, JOE!

Arsenal Women are competing in the Champions League this season, thanks to a third-placed finish in the Women's Super League, in previous manager Joe Montemurro's last season in charge.

The Australian decided to step down after three and a half years as Gunners manager, during which he won the League Cup in 2018 and then the WSL league title the following season. The team also reached three other domestic cup finals during his tenure, and played some fantastic, attacking football throughout that time.

"I want to thank everyone who gave me, a childhood Arsenal fan, the opportunity to be in the inner sanctum of one of the greatest clubs in the world," Joe said. "Not many people get the opportunity to do that.

"But to also be able to lead this team, to have an impact on them and leave something behind – to me, at least – is even more special.

"It's been tough to step away from a club that I have loved so much throughout my whole life. But as a fan, I know it's the right one, and I'll always be cheering for The Arsenal."

CRYPTIC QUIZ

Can you work out what the letters stand for, from the numbers we've supplied? The first one is done for you, good luck!

A 137 = PL CS for DS
PREMIER LEAGUE CLEAN SHEETS FOR DAVID SEAMAN

B 228 = Total G for TH

C 1886 = The Y A were F

D 2-1 = S against C in the 2020 FACF

E 5 = H-T scored by IW in the PL

F 7 = FAC wins for AW

G 19 = SN of NP

H 94 = PL A for DB

I 418 = Total M Played at ES

J 64 = PL G for PEA

K 37 = A of MA when he became M

L 0 = M L by the I

Answers on page 61

SPOT THE DIFFERENCE

There are **EIGHT** differences between these two photographs of the team warming up. The first one has been circled, but can you spot the rest?

PLAYER SPOTLIGHT

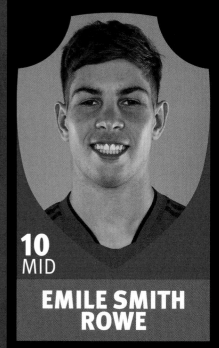

10
MID

EMILE SMITH ROWE

A wonderfully gifted, creative midfielder, Emile made huge strides forward last season, establishing himself as a mainstay of the side. A product of the Hale End Academy, Emile joined Arsenal when he was 10 and made his first-team debut aged 18. But it was last season that the talented schemer really came to the fore. He starred in the Boxing Day win over Chelsea, operating in the No. 10 role, and then kept his place in the side for the rest of the campaign. Comfortable in any attacking position, as well as in central midfield, he ended with four goals and seven assists from 33 appearances in all competitions, and signed a new contract last summer. He also made his England Under-21 debut last season, having been part of the Under-17 World Cup winning side in 2017.

Born: Croydon, July 28, 2000
Nationality: English
Joined Arsenal: as a full-time scholar in summer 2016
Previous clubs: RB Leipzig (loan), Huddersfield Town (loan)
Debut: v Vorskla Poltava (h), Europa League, September 20, 2018 (won 4-2)
First goal: v Qarabag (a), Europa League, October 4, 2018 (won 3-0)

PLAYER SPOTLIGHT

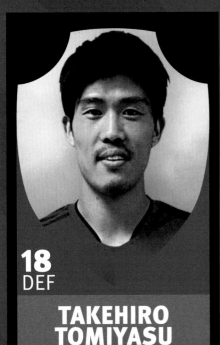

18
DEF

TAKEHIRO TOMIYASU

A regular and dependable performer for the Japan national team since making his debut as a teenager in 2018, Takehiro joined the Gunners from Serie A side Bologna on transfer deadline day. Comfortable at either right back or centre back, Takehiro uses his speed to great effect and has excellent powers of recovery to get up and down the pitch. Starting with home town club Avispa Fukuoka in Japan, he soon became a youth international, having been identified as one for the future at a very young age. He moved to the Belgian league at the age of 19, before earning his move to Italy in 2019 after winning Player of the Year at Sint-Truiden. He spent two seasons with Bologna, by which time he was already a full international for Japan, and had amassed 23 senior caps by the time he joined Arsenal.

Born: Fukuoka, Japan, November 5, 1998
Nationality: Japanese
Joined Arsenal: from Bologna on August 31, 2021
Previous clubs: Avispa Fukuoka, Sint-Truiden, Bologna

HALE END

The Arsenal Hale End Academy has gone from strength to strength over the past few years, producing a seemingly never-ending supply of talented young players - and it shows no signs of letting up any time soon.

From Jack Wilshere and Kieran Gibbs, to Alex Iwobi and Ainsley Maitland-Niles, to Reiss Nelson, Joe Willock, Emile Smith Rowe and Bukayo Saka – the list of stars to emerge from Hale End is as long as it is talented. Home to the club's young players from under-7 to under-16 levels, the academy is a busy, seven-days-a-week operation. Let's take a look behind the scenes....

FACILITIES

There are 197 players based at Hale End, and the various age groups train between 5.30pm and 8pm on weekends, and 10am to 4pm on Saturdays. Sunday is matchday with games kicking off between 10am on 2pm. Each squad from U9 to U16 has their own changing room, as do the officials and there is one coaches' room. There is a restaurant used by staff, players and parents.

PITCHES

There are five pitches at the academy, including an artificial pitch in the indoor dome – The David Rocastle Centre. The pitches are named: East, Clock End, North Bank and West, after the stands at our old Highbury stadium. Each week there are between five and ten matches played at Hale End, and the crowd is made up of the players' families, their guests and various scouts.

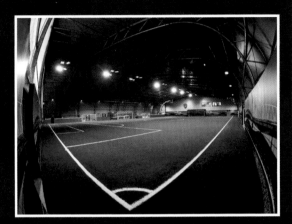

DÉCOR

The walls are decorated in red and white, with photos of academy graduates who have made first-team debuts that season. There is a debuts board listing all of the players who have come through the system, with meeting rooms named after former coaches Pat Rice and Don Howe. The younger players are encouraged to work hard, so that they might be featured on the walls one day.

STAFF

The Academy Manager is Per Mertesacker, and there are also 36 members of coaching staff of the various age groups based at Hale End, as well as analysts, medical and safeguarding staff.

EDUCATION

The club's philosophy is that different schools suit different boys, so all the players at Hale End attend their own schools with the friends they have grown up with. This provides a healthy balance between life as a footballer and a 'regular' family life away from football. The club also minimise the amount of school time the boys miss. Instead of operating a more traditional 'day release' programme, where boys come out of school for a whole day each week, Arsenal now run an early training session at 3pm for each age group between U12 and U16 on one afternoon per week. The club run a drop-in study session on those afternoons so that boys who arrive early can complete work from their own schools.

STANDARDS

When players arrive at Hale End, they are reminded that they are representing the club, so they all have a code of conduct they must abide by. They are to be polite, well behaved to everyone and listen to their coaches. Players all wear adidas boots supplied.

YOUNG GUNS

These three all came through the Hale End Academy and made their first-team debuts last season...

FOLARIN BALOGUN
FORWARD

Born: New York, USA, July 3, 2001
Debut: v Dundalk (H), Europa League, October 29, 2020 (won 3-0)

A clinical forward who has been prolific at every age group since joining our academy aged just nine, Folarin finally burst on to the first-team scene last season. He came on as a substitute in our 3-0 Europa League group stage win over Dundalk at the Emirates, and just a few weeks later he scored his first senior goal for the club, away to Molde. His second goal came away to Dundalk and he made six appearances in all for Mikel Arteta's side during 2020/21, signing a new long-term contract at the end of the campaign. Revealing what fans can expect from him in future, he promised: "They are going to see lots of energy, and I'd like to say lots of goals too." Although born in USA, Folarin is eligible for England, and has played internationally at youth level for the Three Lions.

MIGUEL AZEEZ
MIDFIELDER

Born: London, September 20, 2002
Debut: v Dundalk (A), Europa League, December 10, 2020 (won 4-2)

A technical midfielder with superb balance and ability on the ball, Miguel looked right at home when making his first-team debut shortly after his 18th birthday. An attack minded midfielder with an excellent vision and passing range, he has been with the club ever since he was five years old, and his debut was reward for years of hard work in the academy. He came on for the final ten minutes of our Europa League group stage win in Ireland, and showed some wonderful touches, giving a taste of what could be to come. "I'm an Arsenal fan through and through," he said after the game. "A lot of us have grown up together, playing for the first team was our dream so it gives us the motivation to try and play together, play as a unit and put good performances on the pitch."

BEN COTTRELL
MIDFIELDER

Born: Watford, October 31, 2001
Debut: v Dundalk (A), Europa League, December 10, 2020 (won 4-2)

Cultured midfielder Ben became the 877th player ever to represent the Gunners first-team when he made his debut against Dundalk away in the Europa League – shortly before fellow Hale End graduate Miguel Azeez was also brought on. And it was fitting that the two should make their bow in the same game – the talented duo both went to the same school, albeit Ben was in the year above. Former captain of our under-18s side, Ben joined Arsenal when he was eight, and has steadily developed as a goalscoring midfielder, who scored on his under-23 debut against Chelsea two seasons ago. A hard-working and skilful player, Ben often trains with the first-team squad, and is an England youth international. "I feel really honoured that I'm at a club like Arsenal where I have the opportunity to be the best I can be. It's a dream job," he said.

ARSENAL AT
EURO 2020

Arsenal had four players at the European
Championships in the summer. Here's a
reminder of how they all got on.

BUKAYO SAKA
ENGLAND

One of the undoubted stars of the tournament, Bukayo didn't feature in either of England's two first group stage games (against Croatia and Scotland) but then burst onto the scene in the 1-0 win over the Czech Republic. He was named man-of-the-match for his performance at Wembley, as England sealed top spot in the group. He kept his place in the starting line up for the 2-0 win over Germany in the round of 16 but was injured for the quarter-final victory against Ukraine in Italy. He returned in fantastic fashion in the semi-final though, sending in the cross for the equalising goal, which was turned in by a Denmark defender. And so to the final, once again at Wembley. Bukayo came on for the final 20 minutes of normal time, shortly after Italy had equalised at 1-1.

With no further goals, the game went to extra-time, then penalties. Bukayo – the youngest player on the pitch, and the youngest ever to represent England in a major final at 19 – was designated as the fifth penalty taker. However Player of the Tournament Gianluigi Donnarumma went the right way to keep the spot kick out, and win the trophy for Italy. England had lost in heart-breaking fashion, 3-2 on penalties, but had given the country plenty to cheer in reaching the final of a European Championships for the first time ever.

GRANIT XHAKA
SWITZERLAND

Captain and leading force in the Switzerland national team, Granit enjoyed a fantastic tournament, helping his country reach the quarter-finals. They lost on penalties to Spain in the last eight – a game Granit missed through suspension – but he was on the pitch for every minute prior to that. They began with a 1-1 draw with Wales in Group A, then suffered a 3-0 defeat to eventual champions Italy, before sealing qualification with a 3-1 win over Turkey. Perhaps his standout performance came in the round of 16, when Switzerland knocked out world champions France on penalties after a 3-3 draw.

KIERAN TIERNEY
SCOTLAND

Scotland exited the competition at the group stage, but Kieran starred in the two games he played. Injury ruled him out of the opening game against the Czech Republic in Glasgow, which the Czechs won 2-0. He was back for the next game, helping his country keep a clean sheet in the goalless draw against England at Wembley. He played the full 90 minutes in the final group game, but couldn't prevent a 3-1 defeat to Croatia, and they finished bottom of Group D.

BERND LENO
GERMANY

Goalkeeper Bernd was an unused substitute for Germany in their four games. Having come through a tough group featuring France, Portugal and Hungary, England ended the Germans' hopes in the round of 16 with a 2-0 win.

20
DEF

NUNO TAVARES

Young defender Nuno was our first signing of the season when he joined from Benfica in July 2021. A powerful, fast, left-footed full back, Nuno had been impressing in the Portuguese Primeira Liga since making his debut in 2019 as a 19 year old. He scored and contributed two assists in that impressive debut, helping his side to a 5-0 win over Pacos de Ferreira. He played at right back that day, but is usually more at home on the left. He also featured against Arsenal for Benfica in the Europa League last season. During pre-season he scored just 24 minutes into his first Arsenal appearance – a friendly draw with Rangers at Ibrox – a superbly-taken goal with his right foot. A Portugal youth international, he has represented his country at under-18, under-19 and under-21 levels.

Born: Lisbon, Portugal, January 26, 2000
Nationality: Portuguese
Joined Arsenal: from Benfica on July 10, 2021
Previous club: Benfica

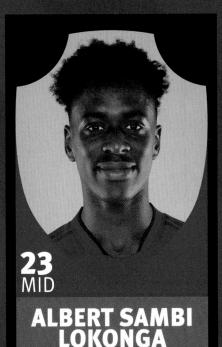

23
MID

ALBERT SAMBI LOKONGA

An industrious, determined central midfielder, Albert joined us from Belgian top-flight side Anderlecht during pre-season, at the age of 21. Born in the Belgian capital Brussels, Sambi (as he is usually known) had spent his entire career to date with Anderlecht, joining the academy in 2014 and going on to make his first-team debut at the age of 18, in December 2017. By then he had already been capped by his country at under-17 level, and he then progressed to the under-21s, for whom he scored twice in his first six outings. He was called up to the senior squad for the first time in March 2021 and has been coached by Gunners legend Thierry Henry when on international duty. A regular in the heart of the Anderlecht midfield over the past couple of seasons, he scored his first senior goals last term – ending the campaign with three from 33 appearances.

Born: Brussels, Belgium, October 22, 1999
Nationality: Belgian
Joined Arsenal: from Anderlecht on July 19, 2021
Previous club: Anderlecht

49

THE MONSTER ARSENAL QUIZ

Twenty-five multiple choice questions – good luck!

IT NEVER HAPPENED

1) Which one of these players DID NOT score 100 goals for Arsenal?
a) Theo Walcott **b)** Robin van Persie
c) Robert Pires **d)** Olivier Giroud

2) Which of these players DID NOT score on their Arsenal debut?
a) Pierre-Emerick Aubameyang **b)** Thierry Henry
c) Emmanuel Adebayor **d)** Ian Wright

3) Which of these players WAS NOT sent off last season?
a) Calum Chambers **b)** Nicolas Pepe
c) Gabriel **d)** Bernd Leno

4) Which of these players DID NOT win an FA Cup for Arsenal?
a) Cesc Fabregas **b)** Kolo Toure
c) Yaya Sanogo **d)** Emmanuel Adebayor

5) Which of these scorelines DID WE NOT record last season?
a) 3-2   **b)** 4-2   **c)** 2-2   **d)** 3-3

ROUND TWO NUMBERS GAME

1) What squad number did Bukayo Saka wear on his first-team debut?
a) 67   **b)** 77   **c)** 87   **d)** 97

2) How many first-team matches did Arsenal play at Highbury?
a) 1,010 **b)** 2,010 **c)** 3,010 **d)** 4,010

3) How many goalscorers did we have last season?
a) 13   **b)** 15   **c)** 17   **d)** 19

4) How many legends are pictured arm in arm outside Emirates Stadium?
a) 20   **b)** 24   **c)** 28   **d)** 32

5) How many matches did Arsène Wenger take charge of?
a) 1,125 **b)** 1,235 **c)** 1,355 **d)** 1,545

ROUND THREE KNOW YOUR HISTORY

1) In which year did we first win the league title?
a) 1913 **b)** 1931 **c)** 1937 **d)** 1948

2) Who did we beat in the 2002 FA Cup final?
a) Chelsea **b)** Manchester United **c)** Liverpool **d)** Southampton

3) Who was our goalkeeper in the Invincibles season?
a) Jens Lehmann **b)** Manuel Almunia **c)** David Seaman **d)** Wojciech Szczesny

4) Who was Arsenal manager when we won the league in 1989?
a) Herbert Chapman **b)** George Graham **c)** Terry Neill **d)** Don Howe

5) At what stadium did we clinch the league title in 1998?
a) Anfield **b)** Old Trafford **c)** White Hart Lane **d)** Highbury

ROUND FOUR NAME THE SEASON

3) a) 1992/93 **b)** 1994/95 **c)** 1995/96 **d)** 1997/98

1) a) 2011/12 **b)** 2013/14 **c)** 2014/15 **d)** 2016/17

4) a) 2017/18 **b)** 2018/19 **c)** 2019/20 **d)** 2020/21

2) a) 1997/98 **b)** 1999/2000 **c)** 2001/02 **d)** 2003/04

5) a) 2001/02 **b)** 2003/04 **c)** 2004/05 **d)** 2005/06

ROUND FIVE BIG GOALS

1) Who scored the winning goal in the 2014 FA Cup final?
a) Olivier Giroud **b)** Theo Walcott **c)** Alexis Sanchez **d)** Aaron Ramsey

2) Who did Thierry Henry break the goalscoring record against?
a) Manchester City **b)** Bolton Wanderers **c)** Sparta Prague **d)** Dynamo Kyiv

3) Who scored Arsenal's first goal at Emirates Stadium?
a) Gilberto **b)** Eduardo **c)** Freddie Ljungberg **d)** William Gallas

4) Who set up Pierre-Emerick Aubameyang's winning goal in the 2020 FA Cup final?
a) Alexandre Lacazette **b)** Hector Bellerin **c)** Ainsley Maitland-Niles **d)** Nicolas Pepe

5) Which of these Academy products was the first to score a goal for the first team?

PLAYER SPOTLIGHT

4
DEF

BEN WHITE

Classy young defender Ben signed for the Gunners in the summer, having enjoyed a fantastic season with previous club Brighton. The ball-playing centre back won their Player of the Season award after a superb campaign, in which he turned in a number of fine performances, missing just two league games all year. It earned him a call up to the England side, and he made his senior debut for his country shortly before being named part of the Euro 2020 squad. The right-footed defender has played in all four tiers of English football during various successful loan spells – the most recent of which was with Leeds in 2019/20, where he was named Young Player of the Season, and helped his side win the Championship title. Comfortable on the ball, Ben is also able to play at right back or in a defensive midfield role.

Born: Poole, October 8, 1997
Nationality: English
Joined Arsenal: from Brighton & Hove Albion on July 31, 2021

8
MID

MARTIN ODEGAARD

After a successful loan spell during the second half of last season, creative Norway international Martin joined the club permanently in the summer. The highly technical attacking midfielder scored twice for us last term – including in the home win over Tottenham – and created more chances in the Premier League than any other Gunners player during his loan. Previously with Real Madrid, where he broke the record for youngest debutant (aged 16 years and 157 days), Martin is already an experienced international, having made his Norway debut at just 15. He is now captain of the national team and was named Norway Player of the Year in 2019, aged 20.

Born: Drammen, Norway, December 17, 1998
Nationality: Norwegian
Joined (permanently): from Real Madrid on August 20, 2021
Previous clubs: Stromgodset, Real Madrid, Heerenveen (loan), Vitesse (loan), Real Sociedad (loan)
Debut: v Manchester United (h), Premier League, January 30, 2021 (drew 0-0)

COMPETITION

Answer the following question correctly to be in with the chance of winning a squad signed Arsenal shirt.

Who scored our final goal of the 2020/21 season?

A. Bukayo Saka
B. Gabriel Martinelli
C. Nicolas Pepe
D. Alexandre Lacazette

Entry is by email only. Only one entry per contestant. Please enter AFC SHIRT followed by either A, B, C or D in the subject line of an email. In the body of the email, please include your full name, address, postcode, email address and phone number and send to: frontdesk@grangecommunications.co.uk by Friday 25th March 2022.

DEFENDING THE BADGE!

Can you find the 18 legendary Arsenal defenders from past and present in this wordsearch?

```
L R S Z C A M P B E L L N U D F
N W J N W E L R Q E N P Q X I G
K I E E R C Y T G O V S F X E
O N E B E V E R M A E L E N O T
D T Y L K O S C I E L N Y I N H
S E E V U M T I E R N E Y R L O
B R Q V W A O M J P A O P E A L
B B A Y N E A N B C O L E L U D
I U A A E U E O R K U R F L R I
G R N D O B U D E E B A N E E N
V N G A T L F O E S A Y A B N G
S P A M D O W Y S R E L D E E A
Y P S S L N U I W U U U N V J T
P G T V L S O M A F C O A D U S
B N R U T R E K C A S E T R E M
```

ADAMS	**DIXON**	**LAUREN**	**TOURE**
BELLERIN	**GIBBS**	**MERTESACKER**	**VERMAELEN**
BOULD	**HOLDING**	**MONREAL**	**WINTERBURN**
CAMPBELL	**KEOWN**	**SAGNA**	
COLE	**KOSCIELNY**	**TIERNEY**	

Answers on page 61

PREMIER LEAGUE
HALL OF FAME

In 2021 the Premier League launched its prestigious Hall of Fame – and two Arsenal greats are among the first eight players inducted.

Thierry Henry and Dennis Bergkamp have both been recognised with the highest individual honour awarded by the Premier League – only players who have retired are eligible.

Here's a bit more about the two Gunners to feature.

THIERRY HENRY

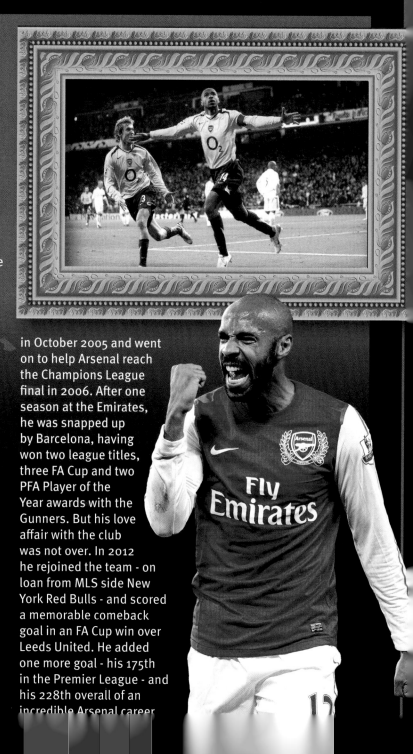

Our all-time record goalscorer, and true legend of the game, Thierry was a world-class forward who thrilled Arsenal fans for much of the Arsène Wenger era. Bought from Juventus in 1999, where he had played as a winger, he was soon converted to a centre forward, and quickly became one of the most prolific players in the game. The Frenchman scored 26 goals in his first season, and 22 in the next, but exploded into life in 2001/02 - winning the first of his four Golden Boot awards as he fired the side to the league and FA Cup double. By now he was establishing himself as one of the very best players in the world and came runner-up in the FIFA World Player of the Year in 2003 and 2004. He was the top scorer in the Invincibles season, missing just one league game in 2003/04 and winning the Golden Boot again. But he wasn't just a great goalscorer, he also contributed a huge number of assists, breaking the Premier League record with 20 during 2002/03. He broke Ian Wright's all-time club scoring record

in October 2005 and went on to help Arsenal reach the Champions League final in 2006. After one season at the Emirates, he was snapped up by Barcelona, having won two league titles, three FA Cup and two PFA Player of the Year awards with the Gunners. But his love affair with the club was not over. In 2012 he rejoined the team - on loan from MLS side New York Red Bulls - and scored a memorable comeback goal in an FA Cup win over Leeds United. He added one more goal - his 175th in the Premier League - and his 228th overall of an incredible Arsenal career

DENNIS BERGKAMP

Quite simply one of the most stylish players ever to wear the red and white, Dutchman Dennis helped revolutionise the club when he joined for a record transfer fee from Inter Milan in 1995. The 'Iceman' took the club to a whole new level, demonstrating a level of technique, skill and professionalism that had seldom been seen in England to that point. In just his third season in London he was named Footballer of the Year as he led us to our first league and FA Cup double for 27 years. A gifted goal creator as well as goalscorer, he specialised in pinpoint throughballs, as well as exceptional goals, operating in the Number 10 role just behind the strikers. He forged dynamic partnerships with Ian Wright, Nicolas Anelka and Thierry Henry during 11 magnificent seasons with the club, and still holds the club record for most overall assists in the Premier League (94). He won the BBC Match of the Day Goal of the Season award twice - first for a superb goal to seal an incredible hat-trick away to Leicester in 1997, and the second for a mesmeric turn and finish against Newcastle in 2002. The latter was recently voted the best goal in the history of the Premier League. He scored 120 times in all competitions, winning three league titles and four FA Cups before retiring in 2006. The first ever match at the Emirates Stadium was the Dennis Bergkamp Testimonial, when greats from both Ajax (his first club) and Arsenal came together to honour an all-time legend of the game.

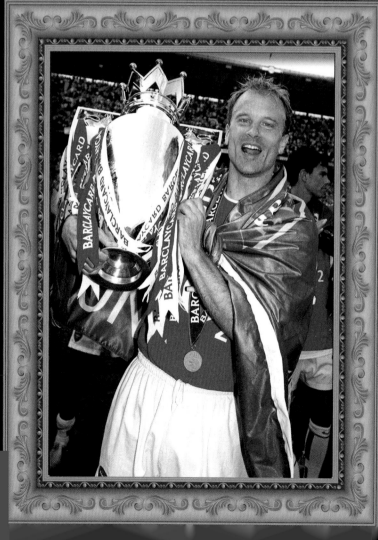

WHO AM I?

Can you work out the current players by the clues given?
The sooner you get it, the more points you earn!

PLAYER 1

I was born on September 27, 1992 (5 points)
My brother is also a professional footballer (4 points)
I scored a free-kick against Chelsea last season (3 points)
I am a Switzerland international (2 points)
I wear number 34 (1 point)

PLAYER 2

I was born on December 19, 1997 (5 points)
I am left footed (4 points)
I scored on my Arsenal debut (3 points)
I am known mainly by my first name (2 points)
I am a defender (1 point)

PLAYER 3

I was born on January 20, 1995 (5 points)
I signed for Arsenal in 2014 (4 points)
I have three England caps (3 points)
I have played on loan for Fulham (2 points)
I wear number 21 (1 point)

PLAYER 4

I was born on August 31, 1991 (5 points)
I have played for Inter Milan (4 points)
I won the European Championships in 2016 (3 points)
I joined Arsenal from another Premier League club (2 points)
I scored on my Arsenal debut (1 point)

PLAYER 5

I was born on March 4, 1992 (5 points)
I joined the Gunners in 2018 (4 points)
I have never scored for Arsenal (3 points)
I am a Germany international (2 points)
I am a goalkeeper (1 point)

MY TOTAL POINTS:

Answers on page 61

UNDERCOVER GUNNERS

Can you work out which players are hiding here?

1

2

3

4

5

6

7

8

Answers on page 61

BECOME A JUNIOR GUNNER!

Junior Gunners is the youth membership scheme, ONLY for Arsenal fans aged 0-16 years.
Our JG Members receive access to a range of fantastic, exclusive benefits, including:

- Discounted tickets to full capacity matches
- Access to free family events
- Opportunities to meet Arsenal first team players
- The chance to be a mascot and part of the Arsenal Ball Squad
- An exclusive Membership Pack*
- Lots of competitions, with prizes such as once in a lifetime experiences and signed player items!

There are three tiers of JG Membership; Welcome to our World (0-3 years), Team JGs (4-11) and Young Guns (12-16).

Each tier has their own exclusive events and competitions, so get involved!

To find out more and to join, head to
arsenal.com/membership/junior

*Full Membership Only

ANSWERS

HIGHER OR LOWER? (PAGE 20)

Cesc Fabregas (212)

↑

Thierry Henry (258)

↑

Dennis Bergkamp (315)

↓

Patrick Vieira (279)

↓

Robert Pires (189)

↑

Laurent Koscielny (255)

=

Tony Adams (255)

↓

Freddie Ljungberg (216)

ODD ONE OUT (PAGE 21)

1. Robin van Persie (the others all won the World Cup while at Arsenal)
2. Santi Cazorla (the others all wore the No.10 shirt at Arsenal)
3. Rob Holding (the others all came through the Arsenal academy)
4. Gabriel Martinelli (the others all scored on their Arsenal debut)
5. Unai Emery (the others have all won trophies as Arsenal manager)
6. Etihad Stadium (we have won the league at all the other stadiums)
7. Alexis Sanchez (all the others scored at least 100 goals for Arsenal)
8. Hector Bellerin (all the others are left-footed)
9. EA Sports (the others have all been Arsenal shirt sponsors)
10. 1999/2000 (the others are all title-winning seasons for Arsenal)

CRYPTIC QUIZ (PAGE 36)

A. Premier League Clean Sheets for David Seaman
B. Total Goals for Thierry Henry
C. The Year Arsenal were Formed
D. Score against Chelsea in the 2020 FA Cup final
E. Hat-tricks Scored by Ian Wright in the Premier League
F. FA Cup Wins for Arsène Wenger
G. Squad Number of Nicolas Pepe
H. Premier League Assists for Dennis Bergkamp
I. Total Matches Played at Emirates Stadium
J. Premier League Goals for Pierre-Emerick Aubameyang
K. Age of Mikel Arteta when he became Manager
L. Matches Lost by the Invincibles

SPOT THE DIFFERENCE (PAGE 37)

THE MONSTER ARSENAL QUIZ (PAGE 50)

Round One - It Never Happened
1. C) Robert Pires 2. B) Thierry Henry 3. A) Calum Chambers 4. D) Emmanuel Adebayor 5. C) 2-2
Round Two - Numbers Game
1. C) 87 2. B) 2,010 3. D) 19 4. D) 32 5. B) 1,235
Round Three - Know Your History
1. B) 1931 2. A) Chelsea 3. A) Jens Lehmann
4. B) George Graham 5. D) Highbury
Round Four - Name The Season
1. C) 2014/15 2. A) 1997/98 3. C) 1995/96
4. B) 2018/19 5. C) 2004/05
Round Five - BIG Goals
1. D) Aaron Ramsey 2. C) Sparta Prague 3. A) Gilberto
4. D) Nicolas Pepe 5. B) Emile Smith Rowe

WORDSEARCH (PAGE 55)

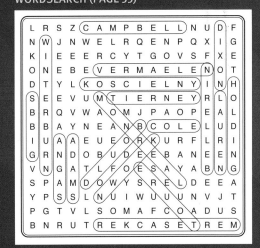

WHO AM I? (PAGE 58)

1. Granit Xhaka 2. Gabriel Magalhaes 3. Calum Chambers 4. Cedric Soares 5. Bernd Leno

UNDERCOVER GUNNERS (PAGE 59)

1. Pierre-Emerick Aubameyang 2. Bukayo Saka
3. Emile Smith Rowe 4. Pablo Mari
5. Calum Chambers 6. Mohamed Elneny
7. Eddie Nketiah. 8. Nicolas Pepe

SPOT GUNNERSAURUS!

1970

mirates to Africa

The Arsenal Foundation   www.arsenal.com/thearse